Healing—

Its Place in Evangelism

by

Edmund Wilbourne

Captain, Church Army

GROVE BOOKS LIMITED

Bramcote   Nottingham   NG9 3DS

CONTENTS

THE COVER PICTURE

is by Peter Ashton

First Impression May 1988

ISSN 0953–4946

ISBN 1 85174 081 3

GROVE BOOKLETS ON EVANGELISM

Introduction to the Series

by Colin Buchanan

The developing pattern of Grove Booklets over the sixteen years since the 'Ministry and Worship' series was first launched has had three standard features:

Firstly, the format and size of a Grove Booklet have remained standard and, as over two hundred titles have passed into print, so the concept has become recognized world-wide.

Secondly, the intention of each Booklet has always been to be practical—starting from a biblical (and usually Anglican) base, no doubt, but exploring the practical features of life, mission, and ministry in the modern world. Grove Booklets do *not* represent some supposed definitive wisdom, or text-book pronouncement. Readers often disagree with parts, but continue to subscribe.

Thirdly, the titles and contents have sprung from virtually autonomous groups, which have had the freedom to work and think under few outside constraints, and have enabled new authors to bring their own contributions into the Christian arena.

When Grove Books became a Charitable Company in 1985, new possibilities opened up. Matters of evangelism had previously been covered in the Pastoral Series—such as the fast-selling Pastoral Series no. 9, *Good News down the Street,* by Michael Wooderson. But now a new initiative was taken by the Church Army to help create a joint group to produce Booklets on Evangelism, of which this is the second. The Series runs quarterly, as does each other Series, and is intended be lively, exploratory, and practical. This particular title picks up a highly contemporary issue in a committed way, and this is typical—authors are not detached scholars, but busy practitioners. Really, the Booklets are intended for lay-people, such as parish groups or training courses, and readers should reflect on what use they can make of them in this way. The Company is very grateful to the Church Army for their part in creating this series.

May they serve God's good purposes.

C.O.B.
May 1988

1. MIRACLES IN EVANGELISM

Introduction
Recently my wife and I travelled with Michael Harper and a SOMA (Sharing of Ministries Abroad) Team to East Africa where we experienced some of 'God's surprises'.

In Tanzania we witnessed miracles and healings as Christians met together and expected God to work. Students at the teacher training college in the foothills of Mount Kilimanjaro in which we were based saw a bright light around the lecture theatre where renewal meetings were being held. They demanded to be let into services too—obviously Signs and Wonders drew them!

Until recently, evangelism in Britain seems to have made little headway. Why the contrast? The principal stumbling block is that British behaviour is dictated more by practical considerations than by theory or dogma. One of Britain's prophetic voices, David Pawson, said that he was disappointed with the evangelism of the eighties. Recent missions in England were almost identical in style with those of the fifties and sixties, apart from new songs. He believes that we are called to go into an outreach that communicates the gospel in words, deeds *and signs.*

I believe that evangelism is essentially 'words and deeds' plus signs. This model has been documented as being concerned with presence, programme, proclamation and power. We have seen the necessity to plan evangelistic crusades but have been unaware of the power concept that there should be in evangelism. I urge that 'signs' are essentially part of the whole package for evangelism.

New Interest
The return of the appetite to a sick person is one of the first signs of recovery. When I first started in ministry, almost 40 years ago, I found that the Church of God was sick, nigh unto death. In the last two decades or so, I have seen a significant change, with the Church sitting up and taking nourishment. The Church that I know is now convalescent and very hungry. As I travel England I am thrilled to find that many Churches are as aware of the Holy Spirit as on the Day of Pentecost, and that the people want to know more about the gifts of the Spirit.

The simple word 'gift' is a good word as it serves to remind us that these blessings cannot be earned but are freely given by God to his children. A gift is not a reward for good behaviour, but a sign of a relationship. Children are given birthday presents, not because they have been good, but because they are children of a family. So people today are interested in the gifts which God gives to his church to enable it to function effectively.

The longing in the hearts of some twentiethth century Christians to return to New Testament days is matched by God who is eager to bring the church of the twentieth century into the same dimension of the Spirit enjoyed by the Christians of the first century, but appropriately, to our age and generation.

Down the Years
Church history is littered with accounts of the supernatural acts of God. St Augustine in the fourth century changed his opinion that signs had ceased with the Apostles when seventy miracles were attested in Hippo during the two years before he wrote *The City of God.*[1]

During the eighteenth century revival, John Wesley recorded in his journal a report of a meeting in Huntingdonshire where adults and children 'Shrieked, swooned, fell and babbled senselessly'. He told the sceptics, 'Perhaps the danger is to regard the Signs too little'.[2]

One hundred years later the founder of Church Army, Wilson Carlile, witnessed what he called Pentecostal blessings.[3] Carlile had started an army of lay people to fight 'against sin, the world and the devil'. The consequence of that battle was that the early history of Church Army is sprinkled with instances of victories over Satan brought about by Signs and Wonders.

Miracles Now
Christians continue to believe that God will reveal his power as they open themselves to him; and part of the evidence is the present interest in the Holy Spirit and Signs and Wonders.

Drawing on his experience of church growth throughout the world, Roy Pointer of the Bible Society says that such phenomena (Signs and Wonders) occur whenever there is an 'Open Heaven' concept. Generally speaking, it is those churches expecting and experiencing Signs and Wonders which are growing fastest. He writes, 'Wherever there is openness to the Spirit and submission to the Word there will be growth'.[4]

Signs and Wonders are an essential part of the proclamation of the gospel. On one occasion, whilst taking a service which was broadcast on the wards at Northwick Park Hospital, I used the set reading from Romans 13; 'So let us put aside the deeds of darkness and put on the armour of light. Let us behave decently, as in the day time, not in orgies and drunkeness, not in sexual immorality and debauchery, not in dissension and jealousy'. A young man, idly listening, sat bolt upright at those words. He had been brought into hospital badly cut after a drunken brawl the previous night. God spoke to him directly, and he set out to find me to tell me that he had received healing and had become a Christian. No one had led that lad to Christ in an approved way.

Many in Britain have come into contact with the ministry of Signs and Wonders through the books, teaching and crusades of John Wimber of

---

[1] From an article, 'Signs and Wonders', by David Williams in *Today* Magazine: October 1986.

[2] *Op. cit.*

[3] Letters to Officers/*Our Quarterly:* c 1908, Church Army Archives.

[4] From an article, 'Signs and Wonders', by David Williams in *Today* Magazine: October 1986.

the Vineyard Fellowships in California[1] and in England through the ministry and writing of Bishop David Pytches of St. Andrew's Church, Chorleywood.[2]

Some Are Critical

Like television 'Match of the Day' highlights, stories of the spectacular can create a false impression that life is a series of wonders. The Athenian in every person dies hard; we love new things. There is a concern by some that Signs and Wonders may:

1 replace the authority of scripture;

2 produce a Gospel without the Cross or repentance and faith;

3 imply a two-stage Christianity of salvation; conversion first then secondly filling with the Holy Spirit.

I realize that Signs and Wonders simply authenticate the preaching about Jesus which evokes a response. While Signs may accompany the preaching of the gospel, it must be clearly understood that the Gospel itself is not salvation PLUS being filled with the Spirit PLUS healing but rather the proclamation of Jesus as Saviour and Lord.

There are dangers, but as the late Bishop A. T. Houghton, of Keswick Convention fame, once said, 'It's the mission of the church to live dangerously'. I say 'Amen' to that! If we don't live dangerously we will never learn anything.

The Essence of Evangelism

The church is the medium through which the gospel is proclaimed to the world. The purpose of evangelism is to 'make disciples'. (Matt. 28.18). A disciple is a learner. I think that there has been a neglect of this making 'learners' in favour of an emphasis on 'making converts'. The question must be, 'What have I personally found as being of the essence of evangelism?

Prayer and Worship

Prayer is the key for all evangelism. I must maintain with all that is within me that the essence of a successful mission is prayer.

And with prayer, I associate worship. This is the worship in which Almighty God is uplifted and we come to him with our heart and soul and mind. John Finney, adviser in Evangelism to the Bishop of Southwell, has described this worship as being, 'not just the golden setting in which the gospel is placed, but as itself evangelistic'.[3]

The lesson that prayer and evangelism are closely related was reinforced when a few years ago on a Mission in the Rhondda, the team decided to spend the mornings praying in the parish church. Before we left the church people were queueing up to see us. Evangelism took place without us being worn out trailing up and down the hills of the area.

[1] *Power Evangelism* and *Power Healing* by John Wimber with Kevin Springer, (Hodder and Stoughton).

[2] *Come, Holy Spirit* by David Pytches, (Hodder and Stoughton).

[3] *Anglicans for Renewal* No 28 page 8.

It is in God-centred worship and believing prayer that people are expectant so that responsive preaching can take place.

The Word, with Signs Following

As we shall later consider, people can be converted when they see the power of God at work in healing. Also, teaching about the Gifts of the Spirit can lead people to expect that God will work through the individual Christian.

Supernatural action of God is proclaimed as being normal in Christian experience. Every New Testament conversion had some supernatural manifestation. This is the basis of power evangelism.

Identify the Gifts

Every congregation must be trained to be witnesses; to witness to its faith. It needs stressing that every Christian has a unique story to tell, that is, their experience of God. This has been called 'narrative evangelism' and it is certainly true that the every-day experiences of the Christian can be the best identification for non-Christians. All are called to be witnesses but not all are called to be evangelists. The evangelist is particularly gifted by God as a proclaimer of the faith. There are a few evangelists in every congregation. The church needs to seek those in the congregation who are evangelists and then to set them apart and train them, and authorize them and use them.

Some churches send out teams of people, often to help another church witness. Ordinary church members of all ages conduct house groups, give testimonies, preach or visit door-to-door and can have an electrifying effect on the parish.

I was privileged to take 40 people from what was then my home parish of St Paul's, Erith, under the Dartford Tunnel to Billericay. The effect on the local congregation in Billericay was dramatic but also the effect on St. Paul's people was that they gained confidence and insights which I would not have thought possible.

What of the Future?

The potential is enormous as Christians tap the vast resources of God through the Holy Spirit in order to fulfill our Lord's command to mission in Britain. The strain is removed as we appreciate that God will work with us and confirm his word by Signs and Wonders. We should expect to see many brought into the Kingdom of God as a result.

Food for Thought

Notice the significance of Luke's words in his introduction to Acts. 'In my former book, Theophilus, I wrote about all that Jesus began to do and to teach, until the day he was taken up . . .', implying a continuing work by Jesus.

'Jesus Christ is the same yesterday and today and forever' (Heb. 13.8).

Read: Luke 24.44-52.

Questions

1. How do you think Christ wants us to make his love and power real and meaningful to people today?
2. What are the 'hidden resources' of God for evangelism?
3. Why do 'Signs and Wonders' appeal to outsiders?

2. HEALING AND THE SPIRIT IN EVANGELISM

Healing in the Old Testament

As far as the Old Testament is concerned, God is shown as a God who is able to heal, 'he forgives all my sins and heals all my diseases' (Ps. 103.3). Not only does the Bible present God as a God who is *able* to heal, but also as a God who *wants* to heal.

God's ideal, and therefore his desire, is that everything would function properly. Little wonder, since God is the Creator of all. When God made the world, including men and women, there was no shadow of disease or sickness, 'God saw all that he had made, and it was a very good' (Gen. 1.31). Clearly, this is the way God intended it to be.

Some time later, God secured that relationship with his people, having set them free from slavery. He said to Moses, 'If you listen carefully to the voice of the Lord your God and do what is right in his eyes, if you pay attention to his commands and keep all his decrees, I will not bring on you any of the diseases I brought on the Egyptians, for I am the Lord who heals you'. So, in the same way as he is the Creator and covenant-keeping God, he affirms his desire to heal.

Healing In the Gospels

Following his baptism in the Jordan, Christ visited Nazareth and in the synagogues announced the special mission given to him by God, to bring deliverance to the captives.

> 'The Spirit of the Lord is on me,
> because he has anointed me
> to preach good news to the poor.
> He has sent me to proclaim
> freedom for the prisoners
> and recovery of sight for the blind,
> to release the oppressed,
> to proclaim the year of the Lord's favour'. (Luke 4.18ff.)

From that point onwards his ministry was directed at destroying Satan's power, and he pressed the battle against sin, sickness, disease and demons right into the enemy's territory.

The sending out of the disciples on an Evangelistic Crusade points to the importance of signs as being part of the mission of the early church (Luke 9.1ff.).

The summit of all we want to know about healing is reached in Jesus. He came not only to redeem peole from sin, but also to reveal what God is like.

Few people think of Jesus apart from his healing ministry. Jesus clearly came to do and to reveal God's will (John 4.34). The records in the Gospels indicate that Jesus healed many people. There are 26 cases of individual healing and 10 cases of multiple healing in the Gospel records. Jesus ensured the future by calling around him a fellowship of people to teach and to train. When Jesus had called the 12 disciples together, he 'gave them power and authority to drive out all demons and to cure diseases. Then he sent them out, to preach the Kingdom of God and to heal the sick' (Luke 9.1ff.). Jesus demonstrated that God was as interested in people's wholeness as is any modern-day doctor.

The Importance of Pentecost

There were many great days in God's calendar—the day of Creation, the day of the giving of the Law on Sinai, the day of Christ's birth, the day of his death and of his resurrection, the day of ascension. The day of Pentecost is also a red-letter day:

> 'When the day of Pentecost came, they were all together in one place. Suddenly a sound like the blowing of a violent wind came from heaven and filled the whole house where they were sitting.' (Acts 2.1).

All God's time changes begin with a time signal

The giving of the Law was accompanied by thunder and lightning. The birth of Christ was accompanied with angelic song. At Christ's death the heavens were darkened, and at his resurrection an earthquake rent the earth. When he ascended, angels announced the news to the disciples that he would return. Now at Pentecost the sound of a rushing mighty wind moves through the room, and tongues of fire appear on every head.

Pentecost was the fiftieth day after the Passover. It was one of the seven feasts that punctuated the Jewish year, and commemorated the ingathering of the firstfruits of the harvest. As God timed the death of his Son to coincide with the Feast of the Passover, so he appointed Pentecost as the time when he poured forth the Holy Spirit.

At the Feast of Pentecost, Jerusalem was crowded with men and women from all parts of the country, and this provided an ideal setting for the descent of the Holy Spirit. As the corn of wheat fell into the ground and died at Calvary, then sprang forth in New Life at the resurrection (John 12.24), so at Pentecost the fullness of that New Life came forth as the beginning of a harvest that is still being gathered in.

Jesus had left clear instructions to his disciples as to when ('in a few days') and where ('in Jerusalem') they could receive the promised Spirit. (Acts 1.5). Doctrinally therefore, Pentecost was the fulfilment of the Great Promise that the Holy Spirit would be given.

He was promised by the Father (Luke 24.49)
He was promised by Christ (Acts 1.8)
He was promised by the prophets (Joel 2.28)

Today through the power and presence of the Holy Spirit we are witnessing our own Pentecost as many Christians open up to receive from God what he gave to the Early Church on the first Pentecost.

The Holy Spirit Is Active in Evangelism

It is necessary to understand the involvement of the Holy Spirit in evangelism before the connection between evangelism and healing can be seen.

The Spirit Gives Power

Christ explained to his disciples to two main operations of the Holy Spirit. He shall live WITH you and he shall be IN you. (John 14.17).

WITH to CONVICT in regard to sin, righteousness and judgment. (John 16.8).
IN to CONVERT to Jesus. (John 16.13).

Then he promised another operation of the Spirit in terms of a new pre-position—'UPON' at Pentecost. (Acts 1.8).

He is UPON us to CLOTHE. He is the Power-Giver in Evangelism.

The Spirit Makes Witness Effective

Prior to Pentecost the disciples were sitting in that Upper Room like frightened sheep in a pen. Suddenly their lives were transformed and they faced the whole city of Jerusalem with the dynamic message of Christ crucified and resurrected.

Their witnessing was not only made possible through the reception of the Spirit, it was also made purposeful in the sense that they had a point of reference who gave power. Christ had not only been raised from the dead, but he had reached the Throne of God—the proof was now both within and upon them. He was truly LORD.

The Holy Spirit made their witnessing positive, purposeful and powerful.

The Spirit Reveals Jesus as Lord

Peter's sermon on The Day of Pentecost indicated a new emphasis and accent on the supremacy and Lordship of Christ.

'Let all Israel be assured of this; God had made this Jesus, whom you crucified, both Lord and Christ.' (Acts 2.36).

Prior to the descent of the Holy Spirit, Christ's name and reputation were in need of urgent clarification to the Jews but the disciples were too fearful to spring to his support. However, all this is changed within moments, following Pentecost. Christ becomes convincing, contemporary and conspicuous by the work of the Spirit.

Healing In The Early Church

With the Gospel records complete, the rest of the New Testament is strewn with evidence that the ministry of healing continued in the early church. Just before he left his disciples, Jesus came to them and said, 'All authority in heaven and on earth has been given to me. Therefore go and make disciples of all nations, baptizing them in the name of the Father and of the Son and of the Holy Spirit, and teaching them to obey everything I have commanded you' (Matt. 28.18ff.).

Jesus gave the disciples marching orders to communicate the Good News of the Kingdom; and part of this was to challenge disease and sickness (Luke 9.1ff.).

The early church took these orders seriously. It is recorded that faith will bring with it miracles. Believers will be given the power to perform miracles; 'They will drive out demons; they will speak in new tongues; they will pick up snakes with their hands; and drink deadly poison, it will not hurt them at all; they will place their hands on sick people, and they will get well'.

I am aware that this passage at the end of Mark is questioned by some scholars. It does not appear in all the earlier translations of St. Mark's Gospel, so in some modern versions it has been demoted to a footnote. Even so, everything in this Marcan extract is confirmed elsewhere in Scripture, and it reveals the practice of the early church.

A Personal Testimony

Throughout the whole of my ministry in Church Army I have always known that there must be more to evangelism than working away at it. I knew that we did not work in our own strength but the gospel was proclaimed through the Holy Spirit. I appreciated that conversion was divinely wrought as a result of the choice to follow Christ. Even so, I asked the question; is there an extra dimension?

If evangelism was only to do with the narrow task of preaching the gospel in words to evoke a response, I needed to ask 'What goes with it?'

Personally, I found these questions answered in 1964 when in praying for a more effective ministry I experienced an overwhelming awareness of the Holy Spirit's renewal. Prayer became a living communion and the Bible an open book. From then on I not only knew *about* the Holy Spirit; I *knew* him. So, Signs and Wonders are now part and parcel of my expectancy in Evangelism.

One of the clearest explanations of the experience of a renewal in the Holy Spirit is that of the Most Reverend Manasses Kuria, Archbishop of Kenya. He explained to Baptismal candidates that they must not confuse the 'Baptism of Water' (which, if they had genuine faith, could be the new birth), with the 'Baptism of Jesus in the Holy Spirit'. He said, 'The Holy Spirit's work is only just beginning . . . many Anglicans have got lost, they think once they have been baptized with water they have arrived, but if you look at their lives, you see they are not bearing the fruit of the Spirit'. He went on to explain that the two baptisms *can* take place at the same time, but that this had not been the case for him. He said 'The new birth which is signified at water baptism is for the unconverted, the baptism of the Holy Spirit is for Christians: it gives you the strength you need to live the Christian life'.[1]

Food For Thought

'God is Spirit' (John 4.24).

For human beings, spirit is intangible. We cannot easily see its relevance. Spirit needs substance before a human willingly responds. God knew this; therefore, he took appropriate action.

Read John 14.15-31.

Questions

1 Can God's progressive revelation of healing in the Old and New Testaments be clearly discerned?
2 Jesus promised power to his followers and said the Father would give the Holy Spirit.
   Is there an awareness and a release of this power
   (a) in yourself;
   (b) in your local church?
3 What do you perceive as the contribution of the Holy Spirit in evangelism?

[1] The SOMA (Sharing of Ministries Abroad) International Newsletter, 1984.

3. HEALTH AND HEALING

In thinking about health and healing, medical science is important. It needs to be said that doctors and nurses are healing agents, whether they recognise God or not. One doctor I know said 'I bandage the wounds, but God heals those wounds'.

Ideally the Church and doctors should work together in harmony. In Ecclesiasticus we read 'Honour the doctor for his services, for the Lord created him. His skill comes from the Most High . . . the Lord has created medicines from the earth and a sensible man will not disparage him' (Ecclus. 38.1-4).

In many cases it is a simple fact that things can be done by medical science nowadays which would have been regarded as miracles in bygone days. We have to face the fact that God does not do for people what they are capable of doing for themselves. Jesus said to the lepers 'Go, show yourselves to the priests.' The priests were the health department of those days. As the lepers turned to go they were healed.

Miracles Abound in Life

For Christians there are miracles for all with eyes to see. The late Donald Gee, a Pentecostalist, once said: 'For those who once received a supernatural healing in direct answer to prayer, one of the biggest human battles is humbly to recognize that sometimes God chooses to bless us with health by the observance of natural laws and strictly regulated tastes and habits—often on the advice of those with skill and experience in such matters. We cling to the supernatural, when God wants, on this occasion, to meet us in the natural'.

Sickness has always been something of a mystery. When Jesus walked the roads of the Holy Land, it was obvious that the healing of the body was almost as vital to his ministry as the healing of the spiritual part of a person which is capable of redemption from the power of sin by divine grace. Many examples are given in the New Testament. He saw with piercing clarity and compassion, the 'sickness' of the whole person, be it physical, mental or spiritual. It is important to remember this, and sad to reflect how the church has somewhat neglected this breadth of vision, and largely concentrated on purely spiritual healing. The plain fact is that God wants people to be physically healthy, yet it is only in recent years that healing of the physical body has been generally acknowledged. Some people still feel that the church has no direct bearing on human health, and that hospitals and medical centres are completely separate entities. How wrong they are! A partnership of medicine and church has much to offer us all.

Why Suffering?

Jesus's whole ministry proclaimed the fact that sickness does not come from God. Some Christians today talk and act as if sickness did. People will say when ill, 'Whatever have I done to deserve being ill?' That was how they behaved in Jesus's day when they asked the question of someone who was sick, 'Who sinned, this person or his parents?' (John 9.2).

Many reports of healing recorded in the Gospels show that Jesus did not think that either impediment or sickness was good for people because God's plan was for wholeness. Everywhere Jesus confronted sickness and disease. The only times he could not cure disease was where there was no faith. When confronted with faith and sickness, he did heal. Thus,

Jesus's coming into the world brought back the beauty which sin had spoiled and made ugly.

There is a paradox here because I do not imply that lack of healing is related to faith or that God cannot use sickness for his glory. I appreciate that many are bothered because some are not healed and continue to suffer and others die. Although Jesus acted sovereignly in healing every known disease in certain towns and villages he visited, not everyone was healed during his ministry, even though he was perfectly able to do it. Similarly, Jesus may not restore every sick person today.

Writing in *Daily Notes* (Scripture Union August 1987) Raymond Brown, past Principal of Spurgeon's College London, concludes: 'We know from our own sad experience that some are physically restored by this healing touch and others are not. It is part of "great faith" to accept that our work may be finished here and the King may want to bring us to his palace rather than send us out on his errands. We sometimes cling to life as if it were much better here than it is in heaven.' The Bible does not encourage that view. One persecuted seventeenth-century minister, Thomas Browning, asked, 'Do princes dread their coronation days?' Surely not!

Of course, there are a great number of things that we do not know about sickness, but it is not a question mark which hangs over the universe, but a cross. We enquire of God, 'Why did he permit his Son to suffer?' The answer we receive is, 'He was pierced for our transgressions, he was crushed for our iniquities; the punishment that brought us peace was upon him, and by his wounds we are healed.' (Is. 53.5).

Place of Faith in Healing
The greatest hindrance encountered by Jesus is his healing ministry was lack of faith. We are told that he 'did not do many miracles' in his home town of Nazareth,' because of unbelief'. (Matt. 13.58) Lack of faith and unwillingness to obey are obstacles which must be overcome before the church can move in the healing ministry.

In Christ's offer of healing, the principles normally include:
> faith on the part of the one who lays on hands or anoints;
> faith by the local congregation or assembly in which the healing touch is available;
> a measure of faith on the part of the one who comes for healing.

When people acknowledge that they need the touch of Christ to forgive their sins and empower them, his mercy is available for every need, even for healing.

The Good News that Christ came to bring is not only for the life to come, but has a present application to the life that now is. God has made it perfectly clear in the Gospels that it *is* his will to heal the sick. Jesus never prayed for the sick in a conditional manner; he tells us that we must believe that we have received the answer to our prayers even before we ask (Luke 11.9ff.).

Importance of Penitence

Do we need to realize that guilt bothers many people? Penitence or reconciliation is an important item in the healing process because body and soul are closely knit. This is an important principle of wholeness. Before seeking healing either from a doctor or in the laying on of hands, the sick person should examine his or her life and make confession and accept the forgiveness God gives through Jesus. He may want to do this on his own or seek the help of a priest, minister, or a close friend.

Wholeness

Christ's main concern was the total well-being of people; body, mind and spirit. Although arguing that healing has a place in evangelism, I would be the first to stress that evangelism is concerned with the presentation of Jesus as Saviour. Nevertheless, Jesus still heals, and I believe that that is part of the Good News he came to bring. Jesus is the same yesterday, today and forever (Hebrews 13.8).

There has been a growing interest in healing in recent years. Wilson Carlile was one who helped to restore the Ministry of healing to the Church. He believed that healing was a powerful tool for Evangelism. As early as 1923, in a sermon in St. Paul's Cathedral, Carlile said, 'In our Lord's ministry, healing of the body was always coupled with healing of the soul'.[1] He maintained that lack of faith had led to the disuse of the primitive rites of anointing and laying on of hands. Prebendary Carlile welcomed the reintroduction of the Ministry of Healing.

Jesus promised that his followers would be able to heal diseases and sickness in God's name and through the power of the Holy Spirit.

Healing is a miraculous ministry which can best be summed up by being described as works of Signs and Wonders.

During our visit with SOMA to Africa, in Kenya we found the Anglican church had left healing to the Pentecostals. Anglicans associated it with emotion and noise! We were privileged to teach them that it could be included in the normal ministry of the Anglican liturgy.

Michael Harper, in his book, *None Can Guess,* warns against a healing cult growing up in a congregation. He says that there is no need for regular healing services, but that healing should take place in the normal daily round of the church's ministry and, when appropriate, especially in the Holy Communion Service.[2]

Generally speaking, the church worldwide is expecting and experiencing Signs and Wonders. Whenever there is openness to the Spirit and submission to the Bible, there is growth.

We live in a period which has witnessed the greatest movement of the Holy Spirit of God in the history of the world. The worldwide church is now growing at a tremendous rate. More than 78,000 people around the globe are being added to the church each day. The Holy Spirit is on the move. Britain is on the Spirit's agenda.

Signs and Wonders exalt Christ when we preach the Good News of Jesus. We should expect God to confirm the gospel with Signs and Wonders, and people today can be challenged by seeing God at work in healing.

[1] Our Quarterly: June 1923; (Church Army Archives).
[2] Michael Harper, *None Can Guess,* (Hodder and Stoughton).

People still respond to seeing God in action. Why not in the local church?

Having recently moved to North Wiltshire and attending Malmesbury Abbey, I have been impressed that healing is included as part of the main Sunday worship. Those requiring the laying on of hands go to a side chapel. This does not interfere with the liturgical flow of the Communion. Frequently also an invitation is given to any who want to become Christians to go forward to the chapel too. Healing and salvation are seen to go hand in hand.

Food For Thought
'I have come that they may have life, and have it to the full' (John 10.10).

Read Isaiah 52.13 to 53.12.

Here is portrayed the life, service, suffering and triumph of the servant Jehovah. Christians see in this reading a vision of the Suffering Saviour.

Questions
1 Can you find in Isaiah's picture of the Suffering Servant (Isaiah 53) a prophetic foretelling of the comprehensiveness of the work of the coming Saviour?

2 What do you think Jesus meant by the words 'believe the miracles' in John 10.37-38, and why were miracles important for an understanding of the Gospels?

3 What is your experience of personal healing?

4. CHANNELS OF HEALING

In addition to medical science, basically, there are five main channels through which God ministers healing, but these are not mutually exclusive.

Through the Ministry of Prayer
Some years ago I finally rebelled against endless prayer lists for the sick. These prayers tended to be formal, dutiful and voide of confidence that healing would actually take place. The emphasis was that God would supply strength to bear sickness, rather than to give healing.

God wants to use the church as a powerful agent in the fight against disease and sickness.

A specific ministry of prayer for the sick is not prayer that is a testing of God, but is rather giving God an entrance into a situation to do entirely as he pleases. There are two questions which need asking before healing can be effective. These are *'Could* God do it?' and *'Will* God do it?' These are two separate questions.

In healing we act in a faith that is certain, and entertains no doubt that God *could* do it. We can believe that God *will* do it. It is as simple and as difficult as that. In this technological age it is often difficult for us to believe that God *could* do it. It is even more difficult to be sure that God *wants* to do it.

Laying on of Hands and Anointing
The two most familiar channels of healing are the ministry of laying-on of hands and of anointing.

In the laying-on of hands, the hands of men and women are related to the hands of God. It is significant that, although God has no body, we often speak of him with human characteristics; his face, his feet, his arms etc. Some feel this belittles God. Some say that we make God like man. The reverse is the biblical truth. Man is like God. So in the laying on of hands, we have a dynamic way by which power is imparted by God to those being touched. And that is the healing touch.

James, probably the brother of Jesus, writes, 'Is anyone of you sick? He should call the elders of the church to pray over him and anoint him with oil in the name of the Lord. And the prayer offered in faith will make the sick person well; the Lord will raise him up' (James 5.14).

The Bible bears witness to the effectiveness of the laying on of hands and anointing with oil for healing, and so do healing services hel nowadays. Another name for anointing is Holy Unction. Olive oil, previously blessed, is used, and the sign of the Cross is made upon the forehead of the sick person. In anointing, faith is expressed in a definite act.

Spiritual Gifts

The other channels for healing are through the use of spiritual gifts (1 Cor. 12). God never intended his church to run by clever machinery or by human methods, but desired that the supernatural ministry of the Spirit should always be at work.

Gifts of Healing

The gift of healing is a supernatural ministry whereby the recipient is able to pass on to the sick person a flow of healing power for the complete recovery and deliverance of the person concerned. The gifts of healing are for the healing of injuries, handicaps and diseases without the aid of natural means of human skills. The plural 'gifts' suggests that there are various gifts distributed by the Holy Spirit in order to meet the challenge of various diseases. This is logical. Since there are many types of sickness and disease, many types of healing are needed. It is not unusual for some people to be better in dealing with one type of ailment than another.

St. Paul, in his list of the gifts in 1 Corinthians 12, also gives other gifts which relate to the ministry of healing. Let's look briefly at them.

The Word of Wisdom and the Word of Knowledge

Ideally, the word of wisdom and the word of knowledge flow together, as first God reveals the details about healing then gives special wisdom to indicate what should be done. Sometimes in healing services there will be words of knowledge given about certain conditions God intends to deal with in the service. Those with the particular symptoms are asked to respond and go forward for healing.

Faith

This gift of Faith is SUPERNATURAL FAITH. It is the God-given ability to believe that there will be a supernatural demonstration of God's power and ability in healing.

Discerning of Spirits

God preserves and protects his church by this gift. It safeguards the church by discerning in healing the source behind any manifestation, as to whether it is of the Holy Spirit, of the human spirit or of Satan. Thus appropriate action can be taken.

Praying in Tongues

Often when faced with a perplexing situation, and uncertain what to pray in regard to healing, the gift of tongues comes to our aid. Tongues enables prayer to get to the real need of the sick person. When the disciples spoke in tongues they enjoyed a supernatural experience, whereby they were linked to God in a way that produced supernatural power within their lives. The God-given ability to speak in tongues bypassed their intellect and produced a spiritual contact with God as they had never known before.

The Ministry of Elders

Even Anglican congregations can learn not to leave everything to the vicar! Some parishes have eldership groups of men and women involved in ministry alongside their incumbent. Often those with the Gift of Healing will exercise the laying on of hands in the home of the sick person as well as in church.

Through the Fellowship

Christ went about healing and told his followers to continue his healing work and he gives assurance of the inherent authority of the church to heal (Matt. 10.8). There is no limit to what God can do when he has a church which is obedient to his command to heal. A church is necessary, not so much to do its members good, but to let the world see Jesus.

Food for Thought

'Now about Spiritual gifts, brothers, I do not want you to be ignorant'. (1 Cor. 12.1)

Read 1 Corinthians 12.7-11.

Questions

1 Discuss the difference between laying on of hands and anointing. What is the distinction of both?

2 Why is prayer so essential in healing? And what more could the local church do prayerfully?

3 What place do the gifts of the Spirit have in your understanding of healing? What does this mean to you in practice?

5. HEALING IS A SIGN

People can sometimes see in healing a sign that God is concerned about their lives. Healing can lead people to seek God. There is no guarantee though that healing will lead to conversion. In the incident in the Gospels of the ten lepers cured by Jesus, only one returned to say 'thank you' to their benefactor.

A ministry of healing is one way of opening up people's expectation to see God in action. Although I cover ground well trodden by others, I do so to make the point that people will respond to the Gospel when they catch sight of Jesus. Healing reveals God clearly to many.

Healing Services in Missions

A recent Ecumenical mission in Crayford, Kent, involving the Anglican, Methodist and Roman Catholic Churches provided an eloquent demonstration. The Roman Catholic Church was packed for the healing service. It was held within the context of a service of prayer and praise and began in semi-darkness. Prior to the commencement, an explanation was given to the congregation about its purpose. This was followed by a procession, including the 14 who were to minister, (lay on hands). The worship was interspersed with Bible readings from both Old and New Testaments. The third reading from the Gospels was linked with the coming of light, as a candle was solemnly brought into the church, and the lights came on. The Gospel reading was followed by the sermon, and then the laying on of hands. Over twenty people received healing and many outsiders were challenged and some responded to the Gospel.

It is my experience that services of healing should be included in every Mission. People can respond to seeing Jesus healing in their local church. Such a service should be midweek to enable church people to invite guests.

One spin-off is that church people are encouraged to talk about their faith when they have witnessed God in action in their church. People do not feel threatened when being told about miracles happening in church. At All Saints in Reading a Mass of Healing was part of the Mission. The churchwarden received healing and said it had enabled her to be more definite in her witness. Another person added: 'When I met people I used to talk about the weather. Now I am able to talk about Jesus'. Any church should realize that a healing service could be an evangelistic one if established on mission principles.

In the Market Place

If healing is a sign which can lead to conversion it becomes necessary to ask: why should it be restricted to the confines of our Christian communities? Surely healing should be taken on to the streets in the same way as we take the gospel to outsiders?

I have laid hands on people following beach mission services by the Clock Tower in Morecambe. But what about a planned cammpaign to take Christ's healing ministry into every market place?

Christians should visit sick people

My contention that healing can lead to evangelism comes from the knowledge that people are concerned to be well. Most people, believing health to be the most important thing in life, are bowled over when sickness strikes. I must confess that in hospital I myself wondered 'Why does a God of love allow illness?' And then more poignantly I asked, 'Why should it happen to *me?*'

It is at this very point that people can be most responsive to the Christian message of a caring God. Being concerned about the sick is not only the Christian's duty, but also his privilege, enabling him to interpret the message of the suffering Saviour who brings comfort, relief and healing. Without pain, the world would be inhabited by robots having neither feelings nor emotions. In such a world there would be no place for Christ and his Cross. Thank God for Christ's Resurrection, which speaks of mastery over sin and death and hope for sinners and sufferers alike!

It is no uncommon feeling on the part of the Christian that he would like to play his part in helping a sick person to regain health—and why not? We proclaim the good news of the Lord Jesus, concerned with body, mind and spirit.

I challenge all Christians to consider visiting the sick as part of the church's pastoral and evangelistic ministry. I give a few simple guidelines from my own experience. I urge that it is always appropriate to pray with the sick person, and often a Bible reading is fitting.

Children

Don't expect too much interest to be shown in your visit! Play a few simple games with them if they want to. They will appreciate the fact that you have been to see them, and a hand laid lovingly on a child's head can say very much more than words. Parents with a sick child at home might welcome a few ideas for entertaining him.

Elderly People

While visiting an elderly lady whose memory was none too good, I established contact by finding out where she was born and then talked about her earlier days. Old people can remember the past better than the present, and most of them enjoy reliving the days when life was more sharply etched. I told her of one or two things happening in her neighbourhood, and then, just before leaving, suggested we had a short prayer together.

Young Adults

When faced with a young patient terminally ill, we feel like questioning suffering. *The Problem of Pain* by C. S. Lewis offers valuable insight. It can be helpful to say 'let's wrestle with the problem together', and to encourage the patient to talk of his hopes and his fears.

In-between People

People in the prime of life are very deeply concerned about their sickness, and tend to think that nobody else understands. Try to share some experience which shows that you do understand, but without 'up-staging'—it's not a case of saying 'My case was even worse', but of empathy, and of showing that God *does* heal. Don't be gloomy, but if the patient wants to talk seriously, don't make silly jokes.

The Churchgoer
The Christian would probably like to be kept in touch with Sunday Services. Get someone to record a Sunday Service on cassette, but do be aware that concentration can be difficult in sickness, so don't press for a discussion of the sermon unless the patient begins the subject. If the person is a regular communicant, see that communion is available, either from the vicar or the hospital chaplain.

Very Ill People
If you visit an unconscious person do not assume that he or she cannot hear what is said at the bedside, they often can! On occasions I have prayed with people who were unconscious, only to hear them joining in the Lord's Prayer with me!

Hospital Visiting
Many people are shy when they visit someone in hospital. Sheer nerves make them say and do the most appalling things. But keep at it. Like most things in life, the more familiar the easier it becomes. Hospitals are terribly noisy. If you decide to pray, do so with the minimum of fuss and don't embarrass the patient. Don't stay too long as you may tire the patient or annoy the staff. And above all, remember that your smile and manner will say much more than words. Sometimes Christians can take part in hospital services. Don't 'talk down' to the patients who are just as receptive as you are.

I have not referred to the mentally handicapped but everything I have said applies equally to them. Such people respond to the Gospel in a very simple and childlike way, and sometimes put more 'normal' people to shame in doing so.

We should not shirk the task of sick visiting; just as the doctor attends and has something to offer, so with the Christian. We have confidence because we take with us Jesus Christ, the Healer and Saviour. This in itself is a valuable part of Christian witness.

The summit of all we want to know about healing is reached in Jesus. He came not only to redeem people from sin, but also to reveal what God is like.

Challenge to us
In spite of the tremendous upsurge of interest shown in the subject of healing over the past decade or more it appears that the Church as a whole has not really come to terms with the question, 'How does healing fit into the proclamation of the Gospel?' I firmly beieve that healing is an integral part of the Gospel. We all need to be more aware of the fact that the Gospel itself is healing. The knowledge that an individual, however sinful, can come to God through Jesus Christ and find forgiveness, peace of mind, and know acceptance as a child of God, is the beginning of wholeness.

Many Christians are inclined to skip over the promises of 'Power Healing' and 'Power Evangelism' in the Bible. Few are prepared to submit themselves to the Divine initiative, or talk about the results afterwards. To help medical research, volunteers have been willing to catch the common cold, but Christians are often unwilling to submit to spiritual research to test the promises of Christ. In this submission there must be faith. 'According to your faith will it be done to you' said Jesus (Matt. 9.29) and this still applies.

In All Saint's, Portsea, following a renewal programme, I made an appeal for recommitment at the Sunday Eucharist. I put my head down, closed my eyes and prayed, not expecting a response. After a while my wife came to me and asked if I was alright. She said, 'Look, all the congregation have gone forward'. In fact, all the 48 people in church that morning responded to that appeal. Another interesting fact was that we could only get 48 recommitment cards, enough for each one.

The point of the incident is that I could have been so busy praying that I missed the blessing. So I believe that we have got to open our eyes and see God at work. We can all be expectant.

Food for Thought
'All authority in heaven and on earth has been given to me. Therefore go and make disciples of all nations, baptising them, in the name of the Father and of the Son and of the Holy Spirit, and teaching them to obey everything I have commanded you'. (Matt. 28.18ff.).

Read Isaiah 35.

Questions
1 What is the 'everything I have commanded you' of Jesus?

2 Do you see in the healing power of Christ a means of making him relevant to people of our generation? Should we be taking healing on to the streets?

3 Could I do more in the healing ministry of the church? And if so, what and how?

SOME RECOMMENDED BOOKS

Neil Cosslett, *His Healing Hands,* (Hodder & Stoughton, 1985).
Reg East, *Heal the Sick,* (Hodder & Stoughton, 1977).
John Glennon, *Your Healing is Within You,* (Hodder & Stoughton, 1978).
John Gunstone, *The Lord is our Healer,* (Hodder & Stoughton 1986).
Charles W. Gusmer, *The Ministry of Healing in the Church of England,* (Mayhew-McCrimmon, 1974).
Michael Harper, *The Healings of Jesus,* (Hodder & Stoughton, 1986).
Morton T. Kelsey, *Healing and Christianity,* (SCM, 1973).
Roy Lawrence, *Christian Healing Rediscovered,* (Kingsway, 1976).
Roy Lawrence, *Invitation to Healing,* (Kingsway, 1979).
Morris Maddocks, *The Christian Healing Ministry,* (SPCK, 1981).
Francis McNutt, *Healing,* (Ave Maria Press, 1974).
Francis McNutt, *The Power to Heal,* (Ave Maria Press, 1977).
M. A. H. Melinsky, *Healing Miracles,* (Mowbrays, 1968).
Agnes Sanford, *The Healing Light,* (Arthur James, 1949).
Agnes Sanford, *Healing Gifts of the Spirit,* (Arthur James, 1966).
Agnes Sanford, *Behold Your God,* (Arthur James, 1958).
John Wimber, *Power Evangelism,* (Hodder & Stoughton, 1985).
John Wimber, *Power Healing,* (Hodder & Stoughton, 1986).

Grove Booklets
Martin Wallace, *Healing Encounters in the City,* (Pastoral Series 30, 1987).
Michael Botting, *Christian Healing in the Parish,* (Ministry & Worship 42, 1976).
Colin Buchanan and David Wheaton, *Liturgy for the Sick: The New Church of England Services,* (Worship Series 84, 1982).
Carolyn Headley, *The Laying on of Hands* (Worship Series 104, 1988).

Pamphlets
Pamphlets by John Richards, available from Renewal Servicing, Ellel Grange, Ellel, nr. Lancaster, LA2 OHN).
  Notes for Healing Services
  Gospels and Medicine Healers
  Gifts and Healing
  Faith and Healing
  24 Healing Prayers
  Laying on of Hands
  Understanding Anointing
  Why Am I Not Healed?

Relevant
John Gunstone, *Prayers for Healing,* (Highland Books, 1986).
Michael Harper, *The Love Affair,* (Hodder & Stoughton, 1982).
David Pytches, *Come, Holy Spirit,* (Hodder & Stoughton, 1985).
Mary Pytches, *Set my People Free,* (Hodder & Stoughton, 1987).